CHAOS & CALM

CHAOS & CALM

ANGELIKA QUIRK

A Publication of The Poetry Box®

Editing & Book Design by Shawn Aveningo Sanders
Cover Design by Shawn Aveningo Sanders
Cover Art: "Jaune-Rouge-Bleu" by Wassily Kandinsky (public domain)
Author Photo provided by Angelika Quirk
Author Photo Editing by Robert R. Sanders

ISBN: 978-1-956285-76-5
Library of Congress Control Number: 2024915529
Published in the United States of America
Wholesale Distribution by Ingram Group

Published by The Poetry Box®, November 2024
Portland, Oregon
Website: ThePoetryBox.com

a wild ride this life
the ups and downs
and when I fell
you caught me
midair

CONTENTS

Winds from the North, Host of Unrest and Disaster

Fleeting Moments

Bursting into Bloom

Your Voice in the Tick of Sap

☙

THE IMPULSE OF THE MOMENT

TIDAL SONG TO THE RIVER

When your floodgates open
I want to believe in the impulse

of the moment, ride your tides
in an orgy of rippling waters

like a lover caressing me, riding me
unbridled like Valkyries to Valhalla.

I want to sing and swim and dive
through the sun-lit sky of your surface

into your currents. I want to fling
myself into your bed and reclaim

the ritual of innocence. If I could
give up the fear of falling,

of drowning, I could dive down
into your murky depth even when

the sun blinds me or float to your mouth
and spill into the vast sea.

RETURN VOYAGE

I fumbled my way back seeking a path away
from the blinding entrance, awake, naked,
crying, kicking my legs into empty distance.

I craved the softness of my mother's belly, swaying
in the dark, encased in roundness of her womb
where deafening sounds hushed to mumbles
where I felt the stroke of her hand on my body.

I wanted to stay unborn, but when the gates swung
open, I had no choice. I tried to swim upstream
like a salmon, back to conception, back to egg,
to sperm, to nothing and just like a speck evolving
in a dream, ruminate in a place of peace,
not hearing the explosions, the sirens outside.
I cried: *Take me back! I don't want to be!*

But only my shrieks. The nurse looked somber.
She slapped me on my back. I screamed even louder
into her face, into the night. But when my mother
swaddled me in white, took me into her arms,
and sang to me, I dreamed of a cradle:

a beginning
          of earth, of light, of now.

REFLECTIONS

I enter a hall of mirrors
glancing at the multitude
of my shifting images
catching me, affirming
my presence.
There is no escape

from this boxed-in existence,
of here of there. Caught
in a frame within a frame,
my doppelganger winks at me
like a trapped moth flapping
in this prism of light.

What is, what is not?
It's not too late to realign
stars and footings, to fling myself
into my own reflection.

Then breaking the glass, shards
fall apart like my fractured mind.
My hands, my feet cut loose.

I swim towards the sky.
A full moon emerges
over the edge: a giant ball
        shrinking as it rises.

If only I could believe in this ride.

ON THE COUCH

My shrink wants to hear my dream
from last night. I can't remember much.
Reclined on his couch I feel his eyes
undressing me, touching my nakedness.
Will he use a scalpel to cut to my soul?

I only recall the sensation of falling
down an abyss, arms outstretched
like tentacles to catch myself. I reach
for my glasses, my amethyst birthstone,
my self-portrait, and diary as they drift
away. When I finally land, I feel like a tree—
no, I am a tree shedding sap and leaves.

What does it mean? I ask.
*What do **you** think?* he says.

I am weightless, no more baggage?
No conventions? My life floating by?

At home I sort out books, knickknacks,
and letters from lovers going ten years back.
I box them, cart them off.

I feel empty now.
Feet firmly rooted.

I breathe in—I breathe out.

MONOLOGUE WITH MYSELF

When I wake up in the morning,
my thoughts drift
like shadow dancers
        of the night before,
once hiding
        in crevices and corners,
now showing off
on the blank walls of my room.

I need coffee and the scent
of rosemary to face
today's affairs,
        and yesterday's prognoses.

I don't want spirits of the deceased
grinning through the open shutters
        mocking me
and dawn unwilling to give up
        its gauze.

        *

Yet I need a fix: cracks
in my ceiling, smudges on windows.
I wrote a letter to God
        about my psyche running amok,
slipping away last night.
Should I check
in the nearest psych ward,
        the nearest morgue?

        *

At this early hour there is nothing left:
        no patience, no bargains.
Only a broom to sweep
        ashes and dust under a rug.

OUT OF LINE

Strict discipline, my beginning: curtsies
to the teacher, posture erect, pencil in right hand,
but no obedience of my pen, just untamed scribbles,
footprints of sparrows in the snow on a winter day
or starlings probing skies in optical illusions.

My hand, a will of its own, rebelling, testing
the periphery of ordinary circles, like fins
swirling in a tank searching beyond the glass.

When Fräulein Gebhard taught us the perfect "V"
I expanded the lines to a vulture hunched over
criticizing me, my penmanship, my sloppy "P's"
prancing off the straight line, my looping "O's"
slowly descending like the spying spectacles
on my first-grade teacher's nose.

Even today when I doodle on my first drafts with globs
of ink, words scatter on paper beyond margins,

chanting: free will of hand!
                          Freedom of mind!

GROWING-UP PAIN

When he was three, I gave him
a dandelion to make a wish.

He blew stars into the air seeking
rainbows and magic, grabbing
a tiny seed, a puff of windblown sky.

Then he whispered in my ear,
I want to be a girl. Will it come true?

He used to wear tiaras
and dress up in princess outfits.

He still secretly plays with his sister's dolls.
But now he is eight and knows,
                              he is still a boy.

THE ESCAPE ARTIST
WOMAN IN PAINTING

She peers out of her framed existence
into the delirium of bird-sky-clouds
while her distant past looks on.
Brushstrokes of dark limbs, stark, bare,
depleted of leaves and the chirp of birds.
Only sirens now, while limbs like witching
sticks pierce smoky skies.

She wants to leave behind the maze
of crisscrossing branches, of earth, of death
of the burned ground where hemlocks'
brush and bramble no longer crawl.
Only her tendrilled hair still clings
to roots and decay.

She tries to escape from this wasteland,
from the charcoaled remnants
of her bridal gown, her wedding band,
the wooden cradle where she rocked her baby.

Escape from the carcass of her dachshund,
from the smoldering ashes,
and her own choking words.

Another glimpse at the promising sky,
another glance into the light, into
hummingbird wings. She now backs
away from the black patches of her past.
She is ready now to step out
of her frame.

Even the artist cannot
hold her back and keep her.

KLEPTOMANIAC

She stole love and pride and stuck them
like trophies onto the mantle of her mind.

First was the mailman who delivered letters
on Valentine's Day. He opened his bag. She pulled
out his heart and a card with foreign stamps.

Then Pete the drummer whose red hair excited her.
She caressed the inside of his palm, snatched away
his lifeline and posted it on her timeline.

An admirer of nights and dark habits, she stole glimpses
of stars and film noirs through peek-holes in walls.

A thief of rumors and rituals, she dined on tidbits
with neighborhood spinsters and lesbian sisters
of pride parades and ransacked their yearnings
for romance and courtship. A squatter of lofty rooms

and ideas in mansions with chandeliers
and French doors, with foyers and libraries
where in winter she moved to a suite upstairs
searching for mirrors lost in drawers somewhere.

She plagiarized Nietzsche, Goethe, Rilke
when sending messages to God, even though
she no longer believed. On the last page of her journal
she copied all German words that ended in "ch"
like "ich" and "mich," the sound of her lost cat,
hissing, and she pinned them to her bulletin board.

In the end she was left with gadgets and glances.
Her trophies, nesting like swallows, drilled holes
into the drywall of her brain: small openings
squinting at the hologram of her elusive mind.

First Cry, Last Cry

At first pogo sticks and leapfrogs,
then running shoes, then the rat-race
through the maze, through traffic jams,
along crooked fences, at last a cane.

We walk but one way and one way only,
no backpedaling, no reinventing a life,
or an exiled God who no longer watches.

Today I saw rhododendron's pink abundance.
They dazzle, then dangle, yet bloom again
next spring. There is comfort!

A yapping dog not knowing, not worried
chases a ball. We chase after the light
that blinks and moves each time we are close.

We are shadow creatures, our pain scratched
into stones we trip over. Our cries loud at first,
then faint, unrehearsed, unrestrained.
Then slowly fading
                    into numbness,
                                into silence.

Plane Geometry

My life, a travelogue
from east to west,
crosses continents
and timelines.

*

I wonder what formula
can solve this helter-skelter
journey when each stop
on a plotted line
is an unknown?

*

At times my angular attitude
is more than 90 degrees obtuse
as I poke at the curve
of each passing day.

*

As I peruse the focal points
in the ellipsis of my mind,
I often lose sight of my goal,
my last day.

*

I had hoped I could bargain with Pi,
(though irrational, yet lurking
around each circle) to acquire
eternal life like its never-ending digits.

*

I wonder about life: its equations
with too many unknowns. Yet what
would life have been like without
possibilities, without arches,
and expanding circles as it fades
ever so slowly into the longitude
of sundown?

Sixteen Lines of Thoughts

1.   The gypsy looked at the palm of my hand:
   cross-stitched lines, geometry of chaos
   and predicted I would die young.

2.   I hung onto the kite like a kindred spirit
   angled against a foreboding sky.
   A sudden gust of wind, the taut line tore.

3.   I trace my lineage back to 1874
   to my grandfather August Hirsch
   who served the Danish king,
   even though he lived in Hamburg.

4.   My lines are open: my cell phone,
   my e-mail, my Facebook account,
   but no calls, no tweets.

5.   Crowfeet around my eyes,
   runes of laughter. A blink, a flutter.
   I saw the horizon creep closer.

6.   A string tied in a knot, held in both hands.
   First cat's cradle, then the Tower of Babel.
   Then she single-handed destroyed them.

7.   He held out his hand and pulled her out
   of the frigid water into the waiting boat.
   After landing in New York,
   she never saw him again.

8.   She drew a chalk line on the sidewalk
   from her house to the neighbor's
   so she would not get lost.

9. Long lines in front of Timmermann's.
    Food stamps in one hand, she waited
    patiently to feed starving bellies.

10. Her last line: *forgive me.*
    Her first: *help me.*
    Then the priest came for the last rites.

11. At birth they cut the umbilical cord.
    At 18 he was kicked out of the house.

12. He crossed the line when he asked
    for her hand on their first date.

13. A sudden jerk, the leash broke.
    No more arguments about
    the obedience of dogs.

14. The surgeon replaced the artery
    to his left chamber. A new lifeline
    pumping to an aching heart.

15. He cast his line and waited.
    A fish swam by, sheared the water
    with its fins as if to wave hello.

16. A marathon from birth to death.
    A life of curves and hidden tracks.
    And when he crossed the finish line,
    he watched the goal sink
    into the flaming sky.

POCKET WATCHES HIDING THEIR FACES, yet THEY TICK

ETIQUETTE OF SURVIVAL

Maikäfer flieg! Mein Vater ist im Krieg.
Meine Mutter ist in Pommerland,
Pommerland ist ausgebrannt.
Maikäfer flieg!*

After the war we had nothing,
but so did everybody else on our block.
No food, no shoes, only footprints
in the ruins of our city.

Life was simple then: homegrown
vegetables, spoonful of cod liver oil,
yet there was the kick of the unborn
in my mother's belly with the child
of another man in a world of angst
and becoming, all knotted together.

On the black market my sister Ingrid
traded with British soldiers
trinkets of NAZI memorabilia
for sweets and chocolates.

My brother Gunnar played
in the rubble of hollow houses
collecting splinters from exploded
flak shells like shooting stars
from ashen skies.

When I sang of maybugs, fathers
at war, and *Pommerland* burning,
I learned that certain questions
were verboten. Only the hush
of adult voices.

Every day we listened to the radio,
the endless lists of the missing.
Every night we placed candles
on windowsills to guide

[. . .]

German soldiers, orphans,
the lost-in-the chaos, the limping,
the broken-of-hearts back
to their families, their homes.

A simple life then: if the day
was well-served with watery soup
from the Red Cross and potatoes
stolen by my siblings from farms
near the *Alten Land*, and finally,
a letter from a Russian prison:
Papa was alive, this was a day of celebration.

In spring crocuses started to bloom
and there was a breeze from the river.
That's when we believed in the omen
of wind and words that the next day
would be okay!

And it was: Finally, the smell
of *Brahtwurst* and Dumpling.
My sister was born.
My brother Parker returned
from the Western Front.
Papa returned after seven years.

---

* *Maybug fly! My father is in the war.*
  My mother is in Pommerland,
  Pommerland is burned to the ground.
  Maybug fly!

CALENDAR PAGES

I.

January, then February, then my birth
in a city bulldozed into rubble where
hollow houses became my playground.
There were newborns, life, death,
and the cemetery near our house
with mass graves.

But what was before the shovel,
the clods of earth, before the holes
in the ground? What happened
before the arrow, the wound, the guilt,
before the stones on graves?

II.

There are those days and weeks recorded
on pages that want to be crossed out,
banished, burned like books,
like *Mein Kampf.*

Months of snow and icicles hanging
from roofs and door frames, daggers
digging at our very essence. That's
when chopped-up legs of chairs, thrown
into make-shift firepits, were our survival,
and we hunched together, close to the heat,
dreaming of summer and peace, while
Onkel Edde, hauled off to prison, refused
the *Heil Hitler* salute, and I wanted to know
Who was Hitler?

What was before *Kristallnacht*, the first time
my sister saw yellow badges and the word
Jude scribbled on store windows? Was
that the beginning before Auschwitz?

[. . .]

What was before air raids and the whistling
of bombs dropping, before the lights went out,
the shaking of our house, and the screams
of Frau Wolle? Before Herr Genenz was found
hanging from a beam?
                              What was after?

   III.

1965, twenty years later, a new calendar,
a new page marked bright red: my child is born,
a new home in Nuremberg. Her father inside
the Palace of Justice, inside trials and judgements
of Göring and Bormann echoing from brick walls
where he worked every day.

His mother's visit with sabbath candles,
borscht and blintzes, songs and dreidels.
And I took my daughter to the *Christkindel*
market to watch the figurines on the steeple
do their ancient dance—gracefully, forgiving.

   IV.

Calendar pages flash by. I try to wipe out
the past listed on graves and memorial stones,
locked into memory like pocket watches
hiding their faces. Yet still they tick.

Lists

It was the time of bombs blasting, birds falling
off roofs, and broken dolls. A bogeyman stalking
me at night grabbing my ankle.

Then the time of daffodils in bloom, the scent of lilacs.
A season of leaping and rolling down grassy hills.

We survived! Our lives censored
by laughter and cries.

*

Why am I here? Not there? Not across the ocean,
but in a room, cloaked in the business of daily lists.

I peel off layer after layer of my life
from cobblestones to fast lanes.
But time runs out when the rooster stops
or the moon clocks out behind dark clouds.

*

I willed my destiny to my son, but he ignored the call.
I walk in my sleep, but dream when awake.

Survivor of words and hand-me-downs,
I escaped to a place of azure skies
blinding me now, counting my coins and debts,
shredding notes and unsolicited mail.

*

My mother's stories are stored in the membranes
of my arrival, I translate each word into proper syntax.
But I am what I am: a refugee from my German past.

My dreams outlive actions.
I once believed in the power of will.
Now I believe in the chance of circumstance.

GHOSTS

I want to rub their bones with valerian roots,
hear the murmur of heroes and outcasts.

     My mother crazed
     by the impermanence of life,
     opened the gas.

     My stepfather drowned
     his worries in schnapps and gambled
     away his license to drive. Before
     the end of the war, he sank
     the pistons of his ship's engine
     deep into Norway's fjord,
     saving the crew.

I wished I could stitch their wounded pride to their valor,
offer them songs, offer them odes.

     Onkel Hans and Frau Meyer's son
     killed in Stalingrad, entrenched
     inside eroded graves, grappled
     with the distance of home, of being reborn
     if only in the minds of the survivors.

     One grandmother killed in Buchenwald,
     the other witness of Kristallnacht.
     You need thick skin, she'd say and wrote
     in my book, Laughter is healthier
     than rational thought. When bombs blasted,
     she sang, *In the homeland, we'll meet again,*
     and I thought homeland was heaven.

I must pray to them, to their haunting spirits
and in their memory plant pansies and forget-me-nots.

DENIALS

I was only fifteen. Even though he's gone now,
my thoughts still drift in silence, yet in compliance

shackled to some unknown watchman
waiting for another show-down.

This morning when the alarm rings,
I feel a sense of urgency. I stagger

remembering the tip of a pointing finger.
I was never able to dismiss the deceit

in his voice nor his roving eyes when confronting
him after the drink, after I fainted. After

his fingers dug deep, after I lay motionless.
But only denials! Lies! He dismissed it all!

What more is there to be gotten? To be
forgotten? When my memory morphs

into raspy chants of bygones' long past,
I mute its volume and plug my ears

to recall no words, no names, no place.
But then those fingers again, razor-sharp,

again the drink he'd offered me, the blue
velvety sofa he'd carried me to,

then the curtain slowly closing again,
and I hear the rustle of leaves through

the open window. And the inarticulate
lip of a moon is once more descending.

HEIMAT—HOMELAND

I.

What was your country called
where your first words
                 were recorded?
Deutschland? Preußen?
The rubble of the Reich?

Remember? Stories
         of *Hänsel und Gretel,*
breadcrumbs, the lure of the witch?
Then houses collapsed
and your eyes reflected the fear
                 of your mother.

Is this what is called
                 Dein Vaterland?
Where tongues spoke the harsh language
of consonants, where forbidden words sank
                 into murmuring pools.

Wasn't this
         what you called Heimat?
The moor, the oak, your chest
hand carved from solid wood,
your mother's wedding gown,
your father's harmonica,
                 your porcelain doll
that could open and shut her eyes.

What happened to them?

II.

You took but one suitcase.
You, the immigrant who flew west
         across the ocean's divide.

You arrived with shards of your past
and sandblasted glass, then opening
skylights to dreams of stars and stripes.

You thought you wanted
the American way: apple pie,
Sunday football. Cheers! Flags!
You even thought you'd forget
your German words, clustered nouns
and verbs, complex, full of meaning.

But here you are, a hybrid in two lands
fitting in neither here nor there.
A foreigner in your own land
where your childhood garden still chimes
                  in the wind, and you swing
back and forth clinging onto roots
then letting go.

Now you live where hummingbirds hover
sipping nectar from trumpet vines
and lilies of the Nile.
The home
         of your children's children.

Yet shingled roofs and stucco walls
         still exposing all
to a fragile existence of wind, of change,
the only constant in your life.

The Immigrant

I left my home on Niedernstegen
with my passport and dictionary,
but it wasn't enough. I needed a map,
a compass, a sign from above. Not billboards
and roadblocks I couldn't interpret.

Wandering along streets and avenues
along Manhattan's West Side among
brownstones and delis with blintzes
and Reubens, my mouth watered
for *Pumpernickel* and *Leberwurst*.

At a fork in a road, I chose
the one to nowhere in particular,
to downtown then uptown, it always
curved around the block back
to where I had started.

I traveled through cities and towns
along the east coast and west coast
in search of a place where I could grow
roots, but never staying anywhere
long enough to settle.

Now I go back and forth crossing
the Atlantic, frantic in search
of some relic, maybe a lost cause,
or a lost photo of Tuttel my cat,
or a special stone from our front
yard inscribed with my name, my birth.

But buried in the rubble of my past,
it's nowhere to be found.

Coda

My limbs no longer obey the laws
of a dancer's body. Legs once splitting
air in grand jetés, my back arching,
angling toward the silhouette of clouds,
and my arms spreading, ready for flight.

Ready to slide from rehearsal to stage,
I'd float in bourrées to vibratos' violins,
starstruck, transfixed as a moth
captured by the lights.

I left my youth, my 5th position, my worn-out
body, slippers, blisters and bunions
all backstage where I'd stitched together
the tip of my toe shoe over and over, reliving
La Sylphide and *Sleeping Beauty*.

Now creaking joints, flab under my arms,
a slight limp, the stilted turn of the neck
to glance into a rear-view mirror and scan
the stage one more time: the good luck
chants, the *toi, toi, toi's* of the dancers,
the curtain rising, the black hole
of the orchestra pit, then floodlights.

I'm on, waltzing to center-stage.
At the end: applause, bows, roses.

Yet each part of my body, each deja vu
mourning my loss.

RUMINATING

I am rehearsing her funeral, but only in my mind
like figments of my dreams: the ritual of sacraments,
of holiness, of roses, wreaths, and her body in an open
casket. Then leaving through the iron gates of the cathedral,
somewhere in Germany where sneering gargoyles,
hunched over between flying buttresses and pinnacles,
stick out their tongues -- solitary guardians
of lofty absolutions, or the absolute?

My sister has been lying in bed for over two years.
Reciting her obituary to myself over and over again,
I wrestle with the idea of going to hold her hand
when she takes her last breath in her room in her son's
penthouse, once the infirmary of a children's ward.
Her whisper from her bedside inviting the spirits
of chance for a chat, an infant boy or girl, comforting
them with her soothing voice, her smile.

In the darkness of night, when the crescent moon
slides behind steeples, then slices clouds in two,
my mind wanders back and forth wanting to see
Ingrid one last time, yet afraid of her gaunt appearance?
Her pleas to help her die? Fear of my own demise?

The next day along the avenue, chestnut trees
in bloom like white candles greeting bird song
after serenades of sadness. Finally, I buy a ticket
to visit her in Berlin

to sprinkle stardust into her eyes
                          so she can see,
to speak to her in our native tongue
                          so she can hear.

Waiting

Always waiting at a bus stop, on a platform, in line at a check-out lane,
at a railroad crossing, at a red light. In winter for summer,
on Mondays for Sundays.

I waited for two days in the birth canal before seeing the light,
before entering the cradle of life, the flutter of time, before
my mother's breast, her voice, her lullaby.

We waited seven long years for my father's return from prison camp,
for his train from miles away where tracks converged on horizons
somewhere in Russia.

Patience is a virtue, my grandmother used to say when my sister
repeatedly asked, *when will we be there?* Patience then was a hallway
waiting for the doorbell to ring, for his letter, a sign from the Red Cross,
waiting for his words, his hugs.

Always waiting at a bus stop, on a platform, in line at a check-out lane.

Waiting in queues for Holy Sacrament, along aisles joining worshippers
to sing and pray where my mother's casket lay. Waiting for my turn
to place a rose in her hand.

Waiting for balloons to pop, candles to be blown out, for fireworks
on July 4th, for rockets, for ticket tape parades, for Martian rocks
with scripts of our past, of our origins.

Always waiting at a railroad crossing, at a red light.

Waiting online for a virtual room, patiently waiting for the shot
in my arm, waiting for my loved ones to unmask, to reinvent smiles.

Waiting in the airport lounge for the next flight out, for crossing
the ocean again, the timeline to another continent, to somewhere
where chaos knotted to a recent past will be left behind.

Waiting in the wings for my entrance on stage, waiting for rollcall, the plot, the recall of rehearsed lines, waiting for the director's cue for the last curtain call.

Waiting for the ball to drop at midnight on New Year's Eve. Always waiting in winter for summer, on Mondays for Sundays.

A Thousand Burning Lights Circling like Fireflies

New York—Babylonian Glitter

I was so young, so naïve, ill-fitted for life
in a big city, the Babylonian glitter of Broadway,
with people faceless racing by, and high-rise
buildings scraping blue skies.

Here I was, after crossing the ocean, a stranger,
an explorer of uptown and downtown, of dancing
and dating, renting a room in Webster Apartments
on 34th we named *Lorelei Rock*. A residence
for sirens ready to claim new turf, ready to gulp
down the sweet wine of excitement, of love,
only declined by loners lost in the bustle,
the maze, the crisscross map of worries.

At a bowling alley in Brooklyn double-dating
on a whim, with Tony half Italian with sleek hair,
with *Lucky Strikes* blowing out rings of smoke
trying to capture my eyes, but it only irritated them.

Stuck in an elevator with Professor Goldstein,
with his tenor voice, and Schubert love songs,
just for me. I pressed all buttons. Finally, the doors
opened on the fifth floor. I got off. But for days
the hum of strange melodies hovered.

Then I met Danny. He gave me a ticket
to Lewison Stadium: Stravinsky conducting
Firebird. When the creature waved its feather,
his hand slipped under my sweater, I let him, loved it.

It can happen to anybody, it happened to me:
when batons whip the air and winds rise.
When the dance on stage sets you whirling,
you have to give in, you have to love to live
as if your very essence depended on it,
as if this moment, this day were eternity.

JAGGED SKYLINES

I had arrived
in a labyrinth of concrete blocks crisscrossing
   shadows and horizons cutting jagged lines
against a blue sky I had arrived hiding among crowds
   rushing pushing rubbing elbows I had arrived
   an outcast in a city of skyscrapers and pigeons
scrambling for light taxi drivers swearing
   in their native tongues honking slamming
on brakes I had arrived in a city of immigrants Italians
   Irish Germans Puerto Ricans aliens with green cards
sending money home every month I had arrived
   racing crosstown from Webster Apartments
past people pulling carts with plastic garment bags
mumbling beggars rattling tin cans and always
   the same homeless man resting in an abandoned
doorway on top of last night's New York Times

I had arrived
yet wanted to leave when puffs of grey clouds rose
   from grates in sidewalks like ghosts from a purgatory below
and trains rattled by at Broadway and 34th where I descended
   two flights of stairs past the stink of piss and vomit
plugging my nose holding my breath then waiting
   for the downtown express when across the tracks
   a man staring at me opened his trench coat unzipped
his flap then took it out like a snake ready
to strike I turned and ran up the stairs into the drizzle
   a thousand footsteps of rubber boots of strangers
unfolding umbrellas in close pursuit but no sight of him
   his digging eyes his genitals I told nobody
not even my mom that day I wrote a letter
home six pages long nothing about
   my tears my terror
I had arrived

THE TOURIST

I only knew how to say *oui*. I was young.
On the steps to Montmartre a man gave me
sunflower seeds to feed pigeons winging
their cooing dance near my outstretched hands,
my head. His eye, his camera, shooting it all.
But then the payback: he wanted 15 Euros.
I paid with coins and my naivete.

Such is the world, nothing free, except
his flirtatious smile, his *ooh la la's*,
and flickering lights.

Even the sight of the Seine snaking around
Notre Dame, free in the setting sun
but costly what was to come:

riots in the streets, cars overturned,
set on fire, lives lost, gargoyles falling
from the burning cathedral.

So, 15 Euros—a small price.

C'est la vie, he had said.
Nothing free.

Much later, I understood.

Turkish Carpet

To weave a carpet is to dig
a well with a needle.
　　　—Turkmen proverb

She sits behind the loom
stitching tangerine moons
through each hole digging
wells with her needle.

Olive shadow branches
dance around the edges.
Fringes loosen.

The stamen of a single flower
dyed with rose petals,
dried in hot air,
blossoms.

I watch her rise barefooted,
her toes brushing against
weft and warp. She whirls,

a Dervish dancer with seven veils.
The song of a zither rising
into the blue ceilings
of Moorish skies.

THE BLUE MOSQUE IN ISTANBUL

(SULTAN AHMET MOSQUE)

I saw her in the inner courtyard,
whispering *Merhaba*, or so I thought.
I saw her youthful stride,
head-to-toe in black, a narrow slit
for her eyes. Mostly her eyes I saw,
for a brief moment only,
then she looked down.

We both entered, took off shoes,
breathed in the slow-moving
light, the dazzling height
of central dome that only
candles and spirits inhabit.

From minarets muezzins' sing-song
voices echoed, and men crouching
on Persian rugs became dark stones
in the mosaic of ancient designs.

I tiptoed through the soft interior
of prayer rugs, of a thousand burning lights
circling like fireflies. Me, a stranger looking
for the exit with my backpack holding
water and maps and ripple effects

of bare feet, dark eyes, her eyes,
and women behind barriers along walls,
a few without *boushiyas*,
a few without headscarves,
most of their eyes blinded
by the traditions from the past.

ODE TO A CAMEL

He kneels in front
of the Grand Pyramid of Giza,
next to Tutankhamen's Tomb,
snorting, blasting
hieroglyphs into sand
as pharaohs watch.

His hump covered
in brilliant designs
amidst the sing-song air
of prayers, of Ramadan
and my fear of slipping
from saddle to ground
as Omar gives me a hand.

And when the camel stands,
his front legs pushing
hooves against arid land,
I hold on for dear life.

He trots, he kicks the sand,
his head held high,
a haughty gaze,
and pompoms sway.
I pretend to be
of Bedouin descent,
my headdress flowing
in the wind.

Stamping the desert sand,
we follow the valley of ancient tales.
A rush of air like murmurs
from pharaohs' chambers,
like hieroglyphs I cannot read,
like Omar, a stranger to me.
But my camel knows where to go.

When pigeons ascend
from the Sphinx, he safely
brings me back,
spitting into the sinking sun.

Santorini

Punished by angry gods.
White, stark, cliff-hanging
with its ancient myth
of self-indulgence,
of their people of Atlantis.

Born in chaos when Zeus split
tongues, and islands spilled
water across their crater

where we entered the city
of sunsets, cats, dogs,
and mules on narrow paths
zigzagging from the Aegean Sea
to its towering rim. I followed

a group of tourists, seduced
by lights and the clarity
of horizons, up the stony trail.

A bearded monk looked at me.
His crucifix embedded in black
of his robe, his eyes. The smell
of incense, of donkey dung,
of dust, of ouzo. I kept my footing
on the pebbles, on the path.

I never intended the white of my eyes
to reflect the entrance to the cave
houses, nor my iris the blue domes
of churches.

We met the monk again
where the windmill had lost
its momentum. Holding breath
I grasped the olive branch
from Olympia and watched his ring
hypnotize the air into prayer.

A dog started to bark at a beggar
or was it the statue behind?
A stone hit the pavement.
Tail between legs, he vanished
into the shadows of walls,
of crooked fences. We walked

on the marble steps of Oia
until the sun looped
behind the last hill, merely
sinking, merely leaving
a memory aflame.

We ate *tiropitas*, sipped liquor
from half-filled glasses
and collected small-talk. In the dark

the tender took us back
to the ship anchored in the crater
where its story had begun.

CRUISING THE DANUBE

Pleasure seekers, geezers, gawkers, hipsters, imposters,
on a boat, on a trip, cruising downriver.

We sit mid-ship sipping red wine and laughter.
A gypsy girl flirts with her lover from Melk to Vienna,
past monasteries where monks had dug tunnels to nunneries.

Let's leave behind the mist of Middle Ages. Let's roam
the hills of the Viennese Woods where Beethoven lost
his hearing but found Elise, where winds rustle
with ancient gossip from canopies to sky to castle.

River of blue waves she flows, she heaves, she sighs,
she waltzes by. I yearn for *Linzer Torte* in coffee houses,
for Viennese balls and try to grasp the essence of loss.

Merrymakers, sun-worshippers, widows, spinsters
with tickets to the end of the trip, to the mouth of the river.
They float along and lounge listening to their own chatter,
inhaling Bloody Marys, rumors, and the rush of the river.

That's when we heard the gypsy's sad story: after her lover
had left her for the redhead, the one with the voice
of a canary, she decided to get off before sorrow
would swallow her and pull her under,
before shipwrecked, before the end
of the journey, before the Black Sea.

Kafkaesque Prague, 2018

The day we lost our way in the alleys
of the Jewish Quarter, wandering
from one synagogue to another,
we listened to the rollcall of the dead
from walls and halls announcing
victims of the Holocaust.

We heard moans from the Moldau,
from arches, the plazas, the towers
where chimes clocked in the hour.

We needed angels! We needed redemption!
And on the Charles Bridge where thirty saints
stood watch, we rubbed their silver armor
for good luck next to crouching beggars,
their heads touching the ground.

And all this time Kafka's spirit, roaming
past narrow alleys, followed us
along the river, up the steps to his tiny home
at Golden Lane perched against the ancient
castle wall where in the quietude of dusk
Metamorphosis escaped, and Kafka slithered
downriver after midnight running away
from the characters of his own creation.

Between the Church of the Holy Spirit
and Spanish Synagogue he now sits
piggy-back on the shoulders of a headless giant,
in his black suit and bowler, his gaze
fixed pointing a finger straight at us.

That night I dreamed of a giant cockroach
crawling into my bed, and when I screamed,
Kafka whispered in my ear:
                    Murder me! Murder me!

LISBON

We walk along the *Rio Tejo*,
past the "singing bridge" to the *Belem Tower.*

He puts his arm around my bare shoulders,
buys *stracciotella* ice-cream for me.

Xales! Xales! A gypsy calls
holding up shawls. She follows

our steps. On the mosaic pavement
I count ochre and pastels.

But when she flashes a toothless
smile, he gives her a ten

and wraps the scarf tightly
around my hips.

White Night Sketches of St. Petersburg

A guard in front of the Hermitage,
one eye black. Quick! Sneak in!
I wouldn't be surprised
if Renoirs could depart
through secret halls!

*

And Matisse' dancers would waltz
along Jordan's staircase,
to the ceiling, out the window.
Brueghel's skaters followed.

*

Then treasures from the basement,
stored among rats and cats,
would flee and float downriver
calling out to you, their star witness.

*

Buy *matrjoshkas*, one giving birth
to another, and amber pearls
from the Baltic. Buy *tsarina dolls*,
fifteen rubels each, and listen to music
from boxes inlaid with stories.

*

Take a glance at a bear cub's dance
to *Valse Trieste* by Shostakovich
and clap your hands with other tourists.

*

White wine, vodka, balalaika songs!
Cheers! *Za nas!* Scoop up caviar and *borscht*.
Drop your black scarf and dance
the *hopak*, the trepak and like Pavlov's dogs
salivate for more.

*

Dostoyevsky, Pushkin roaming
through decades, along windy canals,
their poems blowing to open
hands and open hearts.

*

Join the parade down Nevsky Prospect,
cross your arms, kick your legs!
And when at midnight minutes shriek
and hands point to 12 o'clock,
Baba Yaga flies off
lisping: *Dasvidaniya!*

Winds from the North,
Host of Unrest and Disaster

Winds from the North

This frantic ghost with shifting eyes whips up
havoc, whistling through my chimney
knocking at doors and windows.

What does he want? What can I give to this
wandering spirit, this outlaw rampaging
through halls, thorough ways, and towns
yanking street signs and billboards
from walls to ground where splintered
arms of wooden planks gather
in the aftermath.

What can I do to appease this host
of unrest and disaster? So I can once more
feel the gentle breeze in the rafters and hear
the music of chimes.

What more does he want, this ruthless visitor
from the north hacking at the bond
between house and roof, street and town,
peace and man?

Does he rule with the tantrums of an angry son
or the outbursts of a king or god of chaos?
Is he the origin of everything
                                    or so he thinks?

Sea Shanties

I watched it beach at water's edge barely breathing, waiting for the next wave to carry it back. Its hook removed, gills flinching, fish-eye lenses staring.

*

A horseman gallops toward a sandbank. I think of Goethe's Erlkönig. Then the tide rolls in: waves dipping, crashing. A white skeleton horse riding in on foamy crest with seaweed mane and nostrils whistling in the wind.

*

What is hidden in the depth of ocean floors? The last resting place of shipwrecks, of fishing boats, of rubber dinghies, of *Wilhelm Gustloff* torpedoed in the last days of war with refugees on board from Pillau and Königsberg. Nine thousand dead. Bones white as alabaster, a cemetery thirty fathoms below, visited by schools of fish and flower wreath placed each year into the ice-cold currents of the Baltic Sea.

*

Drowning voices near Lampadusa from boats and rafts. They survived the war in Syria and Libya, left their ruined towns, their mosques, muezzin's singsong voice, their hope, their rituals clutching their belongings in search of peace. When their boat capsizes in stormy seas, two thousand pulled down by twenty-foot waves.

*

A child's body washes ashore. His father clutching him. His eyes turning east toward Mecca.

*

As the moon rises relishing its spit-image on the surface of the deep, I tie a sand dollar and amber stone around my neck and holding a seashell against my ear, I listen to the rush of air.

But all I hear is the echo of a blind sky.

Wilhelm Gustloff, a German military transport ship was sunk on Jan. 30, 1945 by the Soviet Submarine S-13 in the Baltic Sea while evacuating German refugees from East Prussia. 9,400 men, women, and children died.

MAY DAY

He had been hiding underground in his bunker,
der Führer. On May first, they found him
next to his German shepherd—both dead.
Die Stunde null. The hour of zero.

May Day. Parades, protests, banners:
Arbeit macht frei. Work sets you free!
Above the gates of Auschwitz.
In Oakland teachers strike. In Paris people
march from Place Nationale. They scream,
Retire at 62—not 64! Retire at 62!
Molotov cocktails fly, cars burn.
Police with batons. Then tear gas.
Then a stampede. Workers' day!
May Day rallies!

May Day. They raise the Maypole
to an overcast sky. Colorful ribbons snake
from trunk to ground, then flutter in the wind.
Young girls in dirndls grab each strand
spinning their skirts around and around,
weaving their tales for a handsome mate.
The brass band plays, ump tata, ump tata.

Mother's Day! Flower bouquets and cards
and kisses. I display old stapled-together
love coupons of my children with promises
of "free back scratches", and "breakfast in bed".

In a meadow among lupines and poppies
and yellow mustard creeping up the hill,
I discover a calypso orchid in full bloom.
In the tall grass, I inhale the song of May.
My harmonica on lips, I blow in, blow out.

THANKS, NO THANKS

I.

I wasn't asked to be born,
but thank my mother for raising me,
Plato for leading me out of the cave,
the caterpillar crawling along a leaf
for making me feel big.

Orion for putting me back into place.
I thank Goethe, Beethoven, and Bach
for my heritage.

I thank my eyes for seeing
the intricate play of light
in the branches of my plum tree
when the sun bursts through the clouds.

I thank our ancestral fish
that had the sense to leave the water.
I thank the pen and paper for saving
my words in English and German.

II.

I am not thankful for acid rain
and crowded chicken farms.

Passing St. Vincent Drive
with pastures and Holsteins
munching on clover and grass,
I only think of slaughterhouses,
T-bone steaks and plan
to become a vegetarian again.

I refuse to hear news stories
of the plague, the Corona virus.

I don't watch Holocaust movies
and block out the memory of Hitler,
Göring and suicide bombers.

I cringe and wished their souls
were sent to a place far away
to roam in the black holes
of their conscience.

PHASES

Der Mond
He-moon rises above the horizon.
I spy on him through my double-glass
window over suburban Hamburg.
A sickle about to slice the sky in two.

Fifteen nights later he grew
full and plump flooding the sky.
Floating over Paris, he yields
to nouvelles attitudes
with a new name

La Lune
She-moon brags, she swells
courting clouds to wear their gown,
mimicking lovers on the Seine
that bathe in her reflection.

Der Mond—la lune
peddler of dark dualities,
lusting mysteries,
on a quest, lost
in a war of personas.

Tonight, in the quiet of my mind,
I will hear again Coyote's howl
at the orange light.

He-moon, new moon, she-moon, full moon
staring back—silent.

Train Ride from Hamburg to Flensburg, 2015

Wheels spin round and round.
Tracks merge on horizons.

He sits across from us, slumped in his seat brooding.
He says he's on his way to his brother in Sweden.
His home in Aleppo now in rubble.

Squealing breaks at each station,
each town. Then whistles blow.

A conductor in uniform enters, checks his papers.
Thoughts flash through my mind.
Are his papers intact? Will he be arrested?
Two worlds far apart, yet for a moment their eyes lock.
Then the conductor moves on.

Pistons clanking, wheels rattling,
landscapes whizzing by.

A 2nd class compartment on an express train,
no vacancies, crowded with refugees, with sorrows,
with hopes, on their way to a country where winters
are white and words of unknown origins.

We can hardly understand his English,
a few phrases and the alphabet of gestures.
Then he closes his eyes again.

Carriage after carriage connecting
1st to 2nd class, engine to caboose.

Backpacks stuffed with bundles of clothes, of worries,
of memories. The sun of Syria scratched onto their skin.
Mostly men, except for one woman, her child slung to her body
like an appendage.

Trains speeding, wheeling from Hamburg
to Flensburg to Stockholm, its final destination.

They fled by boat, by train, on foot to Izmar
on the Aegean Coast. Then on rubber dinghies
to a Greek island where orphaned children waited
and wept. From Budapest to Austria in torrential rains.
Finally, a train from Vienna to Munich to welcome signs,
unlike during Hitler's Third Reich.

Trains crossing borders, bridges, rolling
through tunnels, through time-zones.

He proudly points at his barber tools in his backpack,
no longer useful in his native land,
where men grow beards now, he says.
He dreams of his own shop in Stockholm
cutting hair and trimming beards again.

Stations, destinations, destiny's last stop
for some in a new town? A new life?

I look around. Are we the only Germans on this train?
Then we pull into the station. We get off and stroll
along the *Fußgängerzohne*, where not long ago
Danish tourists came to buy Bier and Schnapps.

Engines throb, pistons pop,
the heartbeat of minutes and hours,
of hope and schedules.

This time we see refugees in Flensburg.
We think of the man that sat across from us.
For a brief moment only, our lives touched.
Will he reach his brother in Stockholm?
I didn't get his name.

CAGES

Headline:
*Parents of 545 Children Separated At US-Mexico Border
Still Can't Be Found, Oct. 21, 2020*

It's another year.
I'm walking along fences that remind me of borders,
of walls of brick and mortar, of martyrs, of mothers,
sons, and daughters that remind me of voices
of children. Their eyes staring.

Dragged from mothers, herded into cages,
their hands cling to padlocked entries
and cyclone fences. I hear their cries.

Counting back months, days of separation,
their snapshots posted on newspaper pages,
a picture of a baby nameless.
Four years later still waiting
for her mother.

Headlines gone, photos gone.
Our voices numb.
Their plight, their search
of no consequence to us?

It's another year.
I'm walking along fences that remind me of borders,
of walls, of brick, and mortar, of martyrs, of mothers,
sons, and daughters that remind me of voices
of children. Their eyes, their cries, their faces branded
into my conscience.

THEY ALL FELL DOWN

19 dead, 17 hurt.
53 rounds, 36 hits.

They are shooting again.
In back-alleys, on campuses, in fields,
in dance halls, in crowded neighborhoods
where children play and sing:
Ashes! Ashes!
We all fall down.

In funeral halls bodies lie
displayed in open coffins.

19 dead!
We flee, back to our suburbs, back
to the innocence of our four walls.
Doors bolted up, far away from shots
and blood-red rags scattered on grounds.

In Oakland, in Monterey Park 28 shots.
In the fields of Half Moon Bay,
in the shadow of trailer homes,
children play and watch
seven farmworkers fall dead
onto the muddy ground.

Seven wooden crosses,
seven names, seven faces.
Mourners pray next to gawkers
and onlookers. Then church bells.

Jan. 22, 2023 in Monterey Park, CA: 11 killed, 9 injured
Jan. 23, 2023 in Half Moon Bay, CA: 7 killed, 1 injured
Jan. 24, 2023 in Oakland, CA: gang shootings, 1 killed, 7 injured

Corona Rant, May 2020

they say 60,000
dead today
a mugger on attack
where is he now?

a protest march to city hall
hecklers holding signs
they scowl they howl
tattooed ladies in pink
with cherry red lips
they swing they sing

open parlors and parks
cafes and gyms
pry open gates
to trips and tricks

to life or death?
they say 60,000 dead

hustlers and hicks
with red caps waving flags
they chant they pant

open barbershops
bowling alleys
booze and bars

they march without masks
honking horns paying no heed
to disease passing hospital suites
ambulances with gurneys
hearses with bodies
past windows of the sick
the dying

they say 60,000 dead

a daughter a son
their mother gone
no good-byes no flowers
they watched her die
the night before
6 feet apart through
the milky glass of her window
from afar they saw
as her casket was lowered

60,000 dead now
what about tomorrow?

beggars of freedom
they sing they spin

free to choose
breath or death
any distance
far or close

80,000 dead tomorrow

along empty streets
where disease has skipped
to our county seat
and spring has flipped
to summer heat
will fall be next?

blondes with boobs
rednecks with booze
they stomp their feet
they kick they hoot

[. . .]

free to live free to fall
no masks no distance
no walls

yet 2,000 dying right now

November 2020: 250,000 dead
January 2021: 350,000 dead
March 2021: 955,135 dead

BARTERING

I called on the neighborhood of dreams to settle
on my forehead, but I could not replicate
my password, my code. I tried to grow roots
in so many places, but no clods would stick to me

long enough. Now I search for the blink
of my mother's eye, the lip of the moon
as I backtrack my steps to the lost strand
where I began with wobbly steps and single
words making wishes, blowing white fluff
of dandelions in all directions. Now I wish

for the coming generations, offsprings
of loneliness when viruses hit and hid
their contagious faces. When today
is isolation, an exercise of feeble ends
of a thousand hands waving through glass
windows and doors, along corridors

of the sick, the homebound. Would it
be enough now to barter my heirlooms
of wealth and faith for hugs, for love,
for the touch of my grandchildren's hands?

When will we dispose of masks
and fear and distance?
When will we reclaim our smiles
and pin them to our heart?

LACRIMOSA—WEEPING

~after "Bucha, Lacrimosa" composed by Victoria Poleva

In Bucha, in Kyiv, tattered flags
cling to their staffs as houses explode.
In the rubble dogs are digging for bones.

In an orphanage a boy is drawing
stick-figures, then cutting up the picture
with scissors that used to cut his blond locks.
Now they dismember paper limbs.

He is a child. A child from the Ukraine.
He knows war well.

I remember Herrn Ustorf, a war vet
wheeling down the ramp of a sidewalk
his legs amputated. His brother
pushing him holding on to a cane.

I was a child. A child from Hamburg.
I knew war even then.

Who are these dictators whipping up wars?
Ordering soldiers across borders to kill enemies
once neighbors in villages only a few miles
beyond their own country. Ordering
brave men to take up arms, to fight.

Mass graves witness war's rage.
Orphans' and widows' eyes speak!

In Bucha, bulldozed to rubble,
songs rise to heavens:
Bucha, Lacrimosa! Bucha, Lacrimosa!

I once saw Hamburg burning,
phosphorous bombs exploding,
and the silhouette of the sun
in an ashen sky slowly sinking.

I was just an infant.
                    Even then I knew war.

CHRISTMAS, 2023

Early this morning I walked around
my neighborhood in silence: only the flutter
of my breath, white rooftops melting
in the morning sun, and deflated creatures

lying flat on the ground. An angel, a dinosaur,
a Santa once riding on a whale in last night's
glorious parade of lights, no longer moving
or waving, lying still, succumbed
to their fate in flat surrender. Just like hope

in these gloomy days shot down in Palestine,
bulldozed flat by raging war and revenge.
Yet we sang of peace at the *Christkindlmarkt*

and last night on Christmas Eve with my children,
my husband, my grandchildren. We sang
with loud voices with passion resounding
through walls and windows into manger scenes
on front lawns and decorations on roof tops
and trees, in our hands we held bells
and snowflakes like stars plucked from the dark.

We sang in Latin the words of a canon,
clashing with the silence of the night,
until we were hoarse:

Dona, Nobis, Pacem!!
Grant us Peace!!

Will our voices be heard?

WALLED

Stone upon stone
with mortar in-between,
high enough to keep out
neighbors and enemies.

*

Between synagogue and mosque
a wall to wail to pray where a rabbi
slips a note to God into the fissure
of corroded time and stone.

*

Nobody could see her, only her eyes,
hiding behind a barrier, a burka.
During the day she studies
the customs of her ancestry,
at night the strategy of stars.

*

China's Great Wall like serpentine
sauropods crouching, more
than 13,000 miles long.
Its geography of ancient stones
visible from space.

*

My daughter entered
the walled city of Nuremberg
through its ancient gate
to meet medieval *Glockenspiele*
and Dürer's *Praying Hands*.

*

I scaled the *Mauer* between
East and West. A wall
that no longer exists. I saw
the crosses of the deceased

[. . .]

and heard the echo of J.F.K.'s speech:
Ich bin ein Berliner.

*

On a hike in the mountains,
I saw San Quentin shine
in the afternoon sun
like a palace, yet hidden
behind walls, prison cells
and one gas chamber.

*

Walls separate nations,
neighbors, friends.
No windows, no doors,
only tunnels dug
by gophers and illegals.

*

Barriers built, brick-on-brick,
contraptions of mistrust.
Yet songbirds still migrate south
across walls.

They Are Singing

They are singing, always singing on a stage, in halls,
in shower stalls while rinsing their hair. Singing
in a parade among streamers, flags, and well-wishers.
Children with lanterns in a park in the dark, singing
of sun, moon, and stars.

They are singing the *Song of Solomon* in churches, in pews,
in aisles near the cross. They are singing the blues pouring
out their souls. Singing a canon in Latin for Trina's last rites,
Ode to Joy at her mother's wake. Pallbearers chanting
the anthem of grief for children in classrooms shot to death.

Karaoke singers, crooners, swingers bopping heads,
wannabe stars blasting their songs, then raucous claps
or bored looks or yawns.

They are singing *do re mi fa so...* chansons like *La Vie en Rose*
or arias from *Cosi fan Tutti*. Sopranos, tenors, and baritones
in English, in Italian, in German. The Queen of the Night
ordering her daughter to slay Sarastro, the high priest.

They are singing in winter, in spring, and summer.
In the 3rd Reich of *Vaterland* with right-arm salutes
waving swastika flags while Jews were hauled off.
A mother singing her baby to sleep.

Soldiers singing *La Marseilles* along the Champs-Elysees
in a victory march chanting *Vive la France*. Uncorking bottles
of desires, they kiss French girls with red lips and sing along
streets, along the Seine while the bells of Notre Dame ring.

Singing Ukranian hymns on platforms underground, on the stage
of the Met, in ditches of the dead, from windows in rubbled
houses, and from hospital beds. With loud voices, with their last
breath while shots ricochet through the streets and bombs
thunder from above.

Singing, a language understood by all: a lullaby sung
to a newborn child, *Amazing Grace* to a dying man. They sing
until their voices are hoarse, they sing the cradle song of birth,
the fugue of death. They sing as if their lives depended on it,
as if creatures of the skies are calling on them, and in the end,
they break free from the cage, they call life and hear their voices
echo in the bleachers of the skies.

They are singing, always singing.

FLEETING MOMENTS

SCIATICA, OH DEAR!

This morning you woke me up,
Mistress of my Malady! The sting
of your affection for my affliction,
nestling in my hipbone
with such intensity! Oh Dear!

On this gloomy morning
when the chills on roof and garden
hover, I feel your presence, but don't
accept your purpose. Sometimes
I even welcome you when pain

demands my full attention. That's when
I'm no longer moping over the loss
of my looks, my libido.

Sometimes when pain creeps down,
my leg squeezing my heel, I drag
my feet to dance, to tap the planks,
and you disappear, but just for a moment.
Even pills and a letter of complaint
don't help. The next morning
you are always back! Ouch!

It's inevitable, it's unfortunate:
you and I will remain in this state
of elated suffering, a kind of
love-hate conundrum.

What folly to assume there is an act
to follow! What fallacy! What pain!
No band-aids, no massages, no salves
to help! Just pain, Sciatica, oh Dear

MEASUREMENTS

When stepping down a path given to me
at birth or up a ladder chancing a life
not chosen, I calibrate the distance
between rung and reason, dullness
and delirium, sometimes
                    only blinks apart.

Today I dust off my collectibles. If I could
unveil the blueprint of my life, I'd stitch it
to my skin like a rose tattoo and wear gloves
                to avoid its prickliness.

But the given is hidden in lids and lobes,
and when my doppelganger pinches me
on the shoulder on long afternoons, I wake up
                to confront the untold truth.

Sometimes in my dreams, protracted
in units of tosses and turns, I toil with the idea
of cloning golden rules and lace them
to my eyebrows like beams
                of the brightest stars.

I speak only for myself and my predestined path
when I collect flags and floggings each time
I depart, but always come back after circling
                  around the block.

I sum up my life not from square one to dotted lines,
but in expanding circles like horizons widening
and upwelling gyres spiraling until finally I arrive
in the last circle. It bursts like a bubble.
                I am dead, but free at last!

BROKEN

I wished I didn't remember that night:
a full moon piercing my window,
witness to the birthing of my unborn dead.

Timing is everything, my grandmother used to say,
birth, death, and the in-betweens linked by unknowns
in different time zones racing on a downhill slope.

There were three of them—two nameless
before Mia my first-born. One boy aborted,
swaddled in blood and blame.

I no longer want to relive a past sucking
on my breast, my heart, holding on to my breath,
dreaming of my mother's arm stretching
across the ocean.

But death is waiting all around us:
sparrows with broken necks falling out of nests.
I used to bury them under an ancient oak.
Or Frau Örtel's rabbit raised on her balcony
slaughtered at Christmas.

That's when I filled my satchel with petals and roots,
refused to eat meat.

When Mia's hamster died, first one, then another,
she stuck crosses on their gravesites. The next day
she asked, *Will you die? Will I die?*

I did not believe in heaven or eternity.
My parents used to quote Nietzsche, or was it Marx?
Religion das Opium des Volkes. Yet at their funeral
Pastor Hansen read their eulogy.

But I admit I needed a crutch,
so when Mia asked again and again,

[. . .]

Is it true that I will die? Is it true?
I told her of a place in the clouds.

We collected leaves and wrote notes
addressing God. At night we set them ablaze
sending smoke signals skyward.
I held her hand, and we watched
amber sparks like stars ascend.

HE WAS OUTSIDE

~after Wolfgang Borchert's anti-war play, *Draußen vor der Tür*

outside the brick wall   outside the door   the warmth
of room   of floor   where the cold   nipped his lips
and puffs of air rose   outside   with shuffling steps
losing his footprints in the mud   after the war   taking
off his boots   his badge   walking into the river   then
changing his mind   he was an outsider   a clock-stopper
rattler of gates and laws   outside of his mind   of gestures
of kindness   and lucky strikes   a recluse of words
and songs   he was outside   crouching in doorways
freezing   dreaming   of a thousand beginnings

he was   from the wrong side   of the river   the dumpster
disposing of his rags   his rage   his shoes   his memory
even his shadow   tired   hungry   he was ready   to walk
the alleys   the tunnels   dreaming of streets   with open
doors   with entrances   maybe to a church   a school
or a waiting room   at a bus stop   to take off from there
to somewhere   maybe to the girl   who still wore the ring
he had given her   before the war   before she shared her bed
with another man   before she changed the lock   or to take off
from there   to the dealer of dope   to whom he'd offered
his soul   now he wanted it back   in exchange   for his bronze
star   or his pistol   or his kidney   or maybe he could return
to his childhood home   his neighborhood   where his mother
would stand   in the threshold   with open arms
but he no longer   remembered   his own address

Trigger-Bound

He holds the gun to his temple.
(One bullet left)

The power of a single bullet, of his arm
that holds the gun, the finger
that will pull the trigger,
the projectile that will enter his brain
to end his life, his pain, his sorrow,
the scorn of classmates.
(He'll show them!)

When he was six, he owned toy guns
pretending to shoot the bad guys.
No ammo, just pretend.

Now a bullet,
a token to the beyond.
A chamber almost empty
like his room, his last place
to remember.
(Will his mother be sad?)

He turns her photo face-down.
Now is the time,
the reckoning.
(Will he be missed?)

He hears the blast
as if from a distance,
a twirling, a slow-motion sinking

(or maybe rising? To a place in the sky?
Surfing through clouds without
helmet or fear of falling, of failing.)

THE DAY AFTER

At 8 a.m. sharp I cram into my purse
my journal, my keys, some coins.

Quarters, nickels, dimes. I count minutes
like money to be spent before the nurse's call.

My journal entry on page eight predicting
his condition: last night's visit to the ICU,

tubal incisions, his breathing machine
sucking me in, one last time holding

his hand. I take an orange, squeeze
out its juice, swallow the last drop.

My throat resists the urge to choke.
The yellow morning sun digs into

the crevice of the mail slot where
yesterday's news left a shadow

on the oriental rug. I can no longer wait.
I dial, I hear the nurse's voice, *the bleeding*

has stopped—My shallow dreams
of monitors clicking, my heart racing

have seized. No worried eyes should
ever relive the moment before

yesterday, before last night,
before the alarm went off.

OF IMPERMANENCE

I want to die, she said.

Nothing is forever in this fleeting
moment of time and place:
her voice, her laughter, her life.
And soon my memories gone
of the terrace where we sang
of moon and stars late in the evenings.
And a bat circled above.

Nothing is forever even in death,
impermanent like the grave of my mother.
There now lies a stranger, Detlev Palm.
Hopefully they get along. The tombstone
guarded by a cat of clay, also gone.
But the birds in the birch are still chirping.

I finally want to go to sleep
and not wake up again,
she said to me,
but every morning
I am wide awake.

Spirits on ceilings and walls listened,
but stared in silence. Her thin arms
stretched to heaven pleading,
God, why don't you hear me?

Nothing is forever:
her belief, her hope, her God,
transient as refugees from life.

Help me! I still have to sign
my death certificate, she said.

The next day,
God is dead, and I,
I am still alive.

We flew back to San Francisco.
She died three weeks later.
Tomorrow will be her funeral.

THOUGHTS DRIFTING LIKE CLOUDS ON MY MORNING WALK

The sunflower has grown another inch,
its seed sown by the wind sprouting
next to the lavender.

      I was born by chance in the middle
      of winter and war in a moment of passion
      before my father left for the Russian Front.

Next-door *naked ladies* broke ground
overnight, unabashed, from clods
of earth nodding leafless
in pink splendor.

      This morning, I called my sister. Lying in bed
      since her 90th birthday. She said,
      I have eighteen pills left.
      I want to die.

Today I passed the sunflower again.
Its yellow head cut off, only stem left
stretching skyward.

Naked ladies next to the fence.
The caw of two crows.
I stop and watch
clouds drift.

Heartfelt

She felt the flutter of an injured bird inside
her ribcage blurting out its malady
pumping red worries through her arteries.

Sometimes it made plans to escape
into the currents of air, of life, no longer
navigating this downward spiral. At times
warm compresses calmed her nerves.
She even thought of signing a contract
banishing memory's plot to remember.

As she aged, she heard soft murmurs from inside
her heart chambers that lulled her to sleep.
But sometimes she held both hands against
her chest to contain heart's wild thunder,
so it wouldn't fly off before the widening
of chest, the rising of her soul,
the departure in death,

before the raven's return to the roof
screeching all morning long.

INSOMNIA

If I planted pansies on your grave
or wrote this poem to you
would it be enough?

You, tonight again
next to my bedpost
in this pounding storm,
your voice choking.

I used to listen to your breath
and count the ways
you cradled my head.

You are driving in this rain again.
Dead? No tire tracks. You must be.

You hit the tree again. Dead?
No windshield smashed. No blood.

You are. You reach to touch me.
As if the warmth of your hand still is,
just the way it was.

Every morning after
a restless night, the ritual
of brushing teeth, washing face,
of crossing out another day,
another page, and placing
your photo, your smiling face
on the mantle of my mind.
Will this be enough?

To Die, to Live

Along white corridors, the smell of disinfectant, Novocain.
I push his wheelchair down the ramp for the last time,
away from tubal attachments and ticking monitors,
and nurses in scrubs like floating ghosts with stethoscopes
checking his pulse, his breath, his heart. No machines,
no monitors could measure his will to die, to live.
When Father Murphy came to anoint the sick, he gave
my husband not the last rites, but the Holy Sacrament.

*

My father chose to live, to survive seven years in Lager 4736
somewhere in Russia. He listened to the ravens pecking
on white birch like Morse code from home. We lit candles
in windowsills, beacons of hope.

*

After a bout of cancer Tante Helga gave away her possessions:
her clothes to the Salvation Army, her memories to her cousin,
her songs to the wind that sailed through the open window
awakening old voices. She no longer ate, only prayed. She believed
in her fate, the beginning, the end. Finally, she gifted me her ruby ring,
red as the blooddrop from her mouth when she died.

*

He says he wants an orange. I pick the largest from our tree.
I carry it into the house like the sun after a dreary day.
He sucks on it. He inhales the scent, the light,
the promise of another day, another night.

THEY ARE DANCING

They are dancing the tango, the samba, the hula, the mambo,
thrusting legs, slicing air with arms, with tambourines, red scarves,
and fiery eyes. Rocking, bopping their heads, stomping their feet.
Swaying, swooning, lost in the beat.

Dancing in the middle of the world stage filled with confetti
and grief, dancing in carnival parades with red ribbons, batons,
balloons. And on their mother's grave next to a gate.

Tap-dancing on wooden planks, dancing in halls, in barns
in straight lines to a fiddle slightly out of tune. Breakdancing
on sidewalks, in plazas, in alleys in Harlem. Dancing among derelicts
in a park, as bullets ricochet near a bar, as couples dance
at the inaugural ball. Shadow-dancing with the sun, winds blow,
leaves cling to twigs like fugitives waiting for the right breeze.

Some women dance when soldiers return: mothers, lovers, wives.
Others dance on poles in clubs collecting dollar bills in bras,
limbs undulating like snakes, curling up and hissing.

Maypole dances. Weaving strings, celebrating spring.
The Dance of Death in Grace Cathedral along aisles,
below arches, near the baptismal font, near the cross.

They are skipping along sidewalks to follow the piper's call,
his flute, his charm, and in the end they fall, singing, holding hands.

They were dancing when Beethoven sang *Ode to Joy*, when Hitler
wrote *Mein Kampf,* and the *Manhattan Project* was done.
They are still dancing when bombs blast, faces stained with blood,
when shots hit the innocent child. And when they are born:
first cries, then kicking legs.

They touch the sun, then dance on ashes, practicing the graceful
ways of angels. They dance on shards of a broken world.
They dance.

Bursting into Bloom

A ROSE

I graze my dreams of you below
and listen to the cricket's tick,
the quietude of the rock,
and the bee's hum
impregnating a rose.
And there you are
inhaling its sweet scent.

LATE BLOOMERS

It bursts into bloom,
twenty-two years late
after I had carried it home
in a tiny pot of terra cotta.

Twenty-two years late,
an explosion of petals
and shooting stars
moist, sticky

of sap and scent
oozing down the stem.
Its sweet fermentation
intoxicating, after
years of abstinence.

Just like the shiver in my voice,
the yearning for his face
after distance, after silence.

Tangerines

Plucked from winter's garden,
blood-red new moon.

I peel your soft encasement,
hold your membraned secret
in my hand.

Your delicate strings
like fishnet stockings
on the surface of your skin.

Let me taste your winter's crop,
each section, each juicy drop.

Let me suck on you,
squeeze your seedless core,

touch leaf to branch
to trunk to root

and sense your yearning
for propagation.

HALF-LIVED

Not a word, not a sign.
He was gone.
This journey
                half-planned, half-lived
in this phase of waning moon,
now has to breathe in new air.
This restlessness
                when passing his house
now lingers on along corridors
where our lives once touched,
where our snapshots still hang,
but lopsided, empty in color.

I write poems now,
not like a mistress of passion,
nor an ordained minister of love,
but like a lost member of a parish
or a housewife after years of marriage
emptying a bag of dirty socks and denims,
their coarseness clipped to a clothesline
to wrestle with the wind.

                Yes, I live
in this jasmine scent, this summer night
brushing against this past with reference,
with sadness, with dreams:

I want to live without the desire
for him, nor the closeness to death.

THE BOX

Don't tell! It's a secret!
Locked in the lobes of memory,
never to be judged.

July 1   *An owl's hoot in the distance.*
         I climbed out my window,
         crawled along the cascading light.
         We kissed.

                    July 3   *He did not knock. He just pushed*
                             open my window and entered.
                             My wrinkled sheet the only witness.

Aug. 4   *Today he took me for a ride*
         in his red Mustang.
         Don't tell my mother!
         A pregnant moon watching
         our thighs interlocking.

                    Aug. 15   *Alone, in a clinic. They took my baby,*
                              wrapped it, disposed of it.

Aug. 17   *He left an envelope.*
          Inside, a parting note
          and 50-dollar bills.

I folded my secret,
placed it in a box
marked fragile and hid it,
way up in my attic.

On windy nights
shadows jump out
and howl:
Murderess! Murderess!

Match.com

Hearts for rent.
What's your price tag?
Ten minutes here, ten minutes there,
are you willing to commute?

He surfed the internet
for non-committal relationships,
winked at blondes,
the ones with kinky curls,
scanned their images,
and stroked their egos.
Then the computer froze.

Hearts for rent at what cost?
A tear here—a virgin touch there,
or embraces in awkward places?
He grasped the mouse tightly

and clicked. No response.
He clicked again—
she texted him.

The next day when she called,
only his voicemail.

He Was a Musician

On one side the flat moon,
on the other my dream.
Then I awakened
with *Apollo Musaget*.
I cradled his harp,
his song the foreplay
of the breeze.

His hand holding a baton,
that led me on.
His metronome,
the rhythm of my heart.
My skin no longer blue,
but full of apple blossoms.

I willingly opened my lips
inhaling his high C.
My fingers grew
into hydrangeas.
My hair bloomed.

Your Voice in the Tick of Sap

Nubian Ibexes

I look down
through a glass table top
at their twin image,

their curving horns
like crescent moons,
my reflection
half ibex, half woman.

I watch still ears,
hollow entrails,
and their bronze gaze.

Eye to eye we stare
as I conjure a connection
among spirals, myth,
and inspiration.

When darkness enters
through jagged branches
chiseling ibex existence
into segments, into couplets,

a thousand hooves,
first far-faint, then staccato
stampede through
the savanna of my garden
looking for blades of grass,
mulch of leaves.

Thirsty for the drizzle
of November fog,
my tongue catches each drop
wetting the tip of my pen.

BODY PARTS GALORE

Hip replacement on special,
but I'll settle for legs without cellulite
designed by Botticelli. Or better yet
legs with Pavlova feet and Madonna thighs,
fit for stair-masters and musical chairs.

I'll place an order for new hands
with lifelines that extend from palm
to arm with Chopin fingers waltzing
across black and white keys.

In the shop window next-door
new eyes stare at me: blue ones,
radiant, eyes with long lashes,
x-ray visions, and rear-view
mirrors to the soul.

Tongues blurt out: *Price-cuts!*
Price-cuts! Tongues speaking
in metaphoric pentameters
instead of four-letter words.
They click and lick frolicking
across the aisle where mouths
pucker up smacking their lips,
blowing a kiss next to
Munchian screams
and Mona Lisa smiles.
Behind a glass vitrine: mega brains,
Michaelangelo's next to Einstein's
and Sappho's and Plato's
auctioned off to the highest bidder.

A brain on discount in the far corner
with lots of creases in the upper lobes.
Size nine, just right to fit in my skull.

Then I see souls on sale:
some lighter than air,
some thinner than sin.
Souls of popes, of poets,
of dreamers, of angels
hovering overhead.

I wave to them.
One of the souls lowers
its wingtip, brushes against me,

then takes my name tag
and suddenly ascends.

AUTOBIOGRAPHY OF AN ANGEL

Born before time, I consort with other
celestial beings like Gabriel or Michael.
No girls in my family.

I used to count bones in catacombs
of ancient cathedrals. Nowadays
I realign stars and brush
against the forehead of a child
finding solace in her smile.

Once a day I listen to prayers of sinners
granting forgiveness to one, two, or three.
Then back to business grooming
my wings for infinity.

Autobiography of a Sinner

Born to a mother I did not choose,
a father I never knew. I cut off
the head of my sister's doll,
put salt in my mother's tea.
I made up stories about a rich aunt
who would adopt me.

In grade four I was an altar boy.
Let the priest touch me.
Now I tell white lies,
cheat on taxes and my age,
not to speak of infidelity
to my wife, my life, my faith.

But how can I be blamed?
After all, I was born tainted,
without freedom of will.
So, no wonder I no longer believe,
except in original sin.

ANGEL, I WANT TO BELIEVE IN YOU!

Especially during these ashen days.
After all it's not your fault:
      The fires, Paradise lost, your wings clipped,
      your white gown blotched, even your reputation
by a mad-hatter mind or a patient of delusion
or by us who thought you were a mere illusion.
I want to believe in you, even
when you wing your way along
heavenly paths ignoring
      charred hills, dried-out creeks,
      dead fish and earth axis that tilts.
Creature of light, shadowless
are you the spirit of the midnight shift
taking a leave of absence from daily visits?
From sanctifications, benedictions,
from saving children from harm?
I sometimes try to hear your voice
      in the tick of sap, the rustle of leaves
      in my ancient tree that buds each year,
even when crows fraternize
on electric wires and squawk.

I place a terra cotta angel
      on my patio in your image.
The ashes from the fire
once singeing your gown, finally gone.
Your patina now glitters with silver dew,
and when the morning sun hits your face,
      I yearn to possess your grace.

      But when I touch your forehead
there is nothing, only a hologram
of your eyes and empty air.

Postmortem Letter
December 2004

This is to you, Fazah, my child,
hiding in the ruins of your city:

Today I handed in my gun,
my dog tag, my bloodstained
army fatigues. Fallujah's last mission:
Operation Phantom Fury.

I pawned my purple heart
for wings and a white tux,
a hand-me-down from Angel Gabe
discharged for throwing
shooting stars like spitballs
instead of watching over you,
the orphaned child.

I heard the explosion
like a distant thunder:
engines failing, propelling
down, down soaring, ashes
raining from sky window.

Today I arrived, slipping
into heavenly distance.

Fazah, my child,
I will guide you now
to catch fireflies
that ignite into stars,
glowing in the dark.

A Final Dot

On the last page of my journal, I scribble
in faint loopings the uphill and downhill
escapades of my roller-coasting mind.

All this time I've been waiting
for stars to shoot through decades
to the umbilical beginning,
the beginning of my plum tree,
my rose, thorns, hallelujahs, and love.

Now I wait for a voice, an angel, a god,
for something, anything to lead me on.
I wait in my garden like a patient
breathing in the potion of lavender
and sunlight. At night I drink in the Milky Way
to quench my thirst for the calming dark,

and I wonder, *After death—life?*
a new beginning? To meet my mother
somewhere in heaven or become
a raven, a moth, a falcon?

Sometimes I think of the origin
of earth, the universe, whirling,
circling in my head.

But then it stops. No more thoughts,
no more words. Only a final dot
like the farthest star,

maybe Earendel, the star of dawn,
12.9 billion lightyears away.

A blink—into eternity?

Acknowledgments

TRANS-LIT2: "Kleptomaniac" and "Of Impermanence," translated into German, *"Vom Vergänglichen"* (Winner of the *SCALG Literaturpreis*, 2023)

Of Skyscrapers and Pigeons: "New York – Babylonian Glitter," "Jagged Skylines," "Turkish Carpet," "The Blue Mosque in Istanbul," "Ode to a Camel," "Santorini," "Cruising the Danube," "Kafkanesque Prague," "Lisbon," "The Immigrant," and "White Sketches of St. Petersburg," 2022

The Sum of Us: "Monologue of My Self," "Ghosts," "Phases," "He Was Outside," and "They are Dancing," 2019

Marin Poetry Center Anthology: "Broken," 2018

Plainsong (Hastings College Press): "To Die, to Live," Award Poem, 2018

Los Angeles Review: "Of Impermanence" and "To Die, to Live," forthcoming in bilingual versions (German/English)

Special thanks to my poet friends Brenda Gunn, Gabrielle Rilleau, Laurel Feigenbaum, Melanie Maier, and Suzanne Himmelright. I especially appreciate Ella Eytan for hosting our Saturday and Wednesday groups, always cheerful, encouraging, with a keen editorial eye, and Erin Rodoni for her inspiration as poet, her insight, and invaluable feedback.

My gratitude to Tom Centolella for reading my poems, for all encouragements, suggestions, and always helpful critiques.

I am also grateful to Francesca Bell for prodding me to go back to my German roots and translate some of my poems into English.

I am forever thankful to my husband for patiently listening to my poems, attending all my readings, and being my greatest fan!

ABOUT THE AUTHOR

Angelika Quirk was born and raised in Hamburg, Germany. Her poetry is influenced by German culture and the angst of post-World War II experiences. At the age of 18 she immigrated to the United States. She graduated from U.C. Berkely with a BA in German Literature. Her poetry has appeared in various literary magazines including *N.Y. Quarterly, California Quarterly, TRANS-LIT2* and Marin Poetry Center's Anthologies. She was a member of the Marin Poetry Center for six years in charge of the High School Poetry Program. Two of her poetry books, *After Sirens, Of Ruins and Rumors,* and her memoir *Kriegskinder* are in the library of the German American Heritage Museum in Wahington D. C. Her poem, *"Vom Vergänglichen"* recently won the SCALG Lyrik-Preis, 2023.

In a former life, she danced in *Totentanz* at Grace Cathedral in San Francisco and was on the record album cover of the *Schlagerparade 1968* (*Hit Parade* 1968) in Germany. A lover of music, collector of words in English and German, she now writes poems about life and living. Her Leitmotif: to instill emotions and passions from the surreal to the sublime, from chaos to rhythm to rhyme.

facebook.com/angelika.quirk

ABOUT THE POETRY BOX®

The Poetry Box, a boutique publishing company in Portland, Oregon, provides a platform for both established and emerging poets to share their words with the world through beautiful printed books and chapbooks.

Feel free to visit the online bookstore (thePoetryBox.com), where you'll find more titles including:

Inside, Outside by Kirsten Morgan

The Squannacook at Dawn by Richard Jordan

Reading Wind by Carol Barrett

Journey of Trees by Susan Landgraf

White Sail at Midnight by Ginny Lowe Connors

Lamplight by Cathy Cain

Acceleration Due to Gravity by Heikki Huotari

Life in No Ordinary Time by Laurel Feigenbaum

Field Notes from an Illusion by Lois Levinson

What She Was Wearing by Shawn Aveningo Sanders

When All Else Fails by Lana Hechtman Ayers

Nothing More to Lose by Carolyn Martin

Self Dissection by Amelia Diaz Ettinger

The Beautiful One's Ark by Sher A. Schwartz

A Bit Left of Straight Ahead by Kim Peter Kovac

Rescue Dogs by Fred Zirm

and more . . .

Milton Keynes UK
Ingram Content Group UK Ltd.
UKHW050921231124
451587UK00021B/309

9 781956 285765